HUMMiNGBiRDS

Sparkles

A Children's Book Author Illustrator
living in Nebraska.
She has Written and Illustrated 16+ Beginner
Books for Kids. Available @ Amazon &
Bookstores World-wide.

Mission:
Make Reading Fun &
giving Kids Tools to Navigate Life.

Sparkles
BOOKS

Hummingbirds are bright and sparkle like gems.

Ruby-throat

Black-chinned

Rufous

Anna's

The males have a Gorget, which is a flashy patch on it's neck.

Allen's

Most Females

Most females are sparkling green and white with a touch of color.

That's *Amazing!*

3

Hummingbirds are the smallest bird in the World!

Most weigh the less than a nickel. They are only 3 to 4 inches long.

That's *Amazing!*

4

Hummingbirds fly
so fast you cannot
see their wings!

They are the
fastest animal in
the World!

5

Hummmmmmmmmm....

They are called
Hummingbirds
because of the
humming sound
their wings make
when flying.

That's Amazing!

6

Hummingbirds do not flap their wings, they rotate them in a figure 8.

8

Their tiny wings beat up to

200

times per second!

Hummingbirds are the only bird that can fly forward, backward...

...and upside down!

Photography by Barbara
Caballero VanMatre

That's *Amazing!*

8

Hummingbirds can also hover. Which means staying in one place.

Photography by Barbara Caballero VanMatre

Hummingbirds are fast fliers!

They are tiny at just
3 to 4 inches long....

...and they can fly faster than a fighter jet!

Relatively, compared to size.

<u>Speed Measured in Body</u>
<u>Lengths per Second</u>

Fighter Jet = 160
Hummingbird = 380

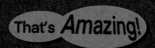

That's Amazing!

Hummingbirds 🖤 love
Flower Nectar!
Which is mostly sugar.

Hopped up on
Sugar!

They can drink
half of their body
weight in Nectar
in 1 day!

That's *Amazing!*

A Hummingbird visits 1500 flowers a day to get the Nectar they need.

Pollinators!

Many plants rely on Hummingbirds for Pollination.

Hummingbirds also get Nectar from Feeders.

Hopped on sugar!

It is a Sugar Water Nectar that is similar to Flower Nectar.

That's Amazing!

14

Hummingbirds are feisty and will fight for flowers and feeders.

They do not like to share and will chase each other for Nectar.

Most Hummingbirds live in Mexico and South America.

MAY

APRIL

MARCH

Some will Fly (Migrate) North to the United States and Canada in the Spring.

16

Hummingbirds fly
thousands of miles
every year!

Find out where
they are now.
Track
Hummingbirds and
Report Sightings!

Go to the Website:
Hummer-News.com

17

The Blooming flowers and warm south wind guide them north.

Hummingbirds usually follow the same migration route every year.

Hummingbirds also use the Earth's magnetic field, stars and landmarks as guides.

That's *Amazing!*

For such tiny birds, they have incredible Navigation abilities.

20

And they usually arrive
on the same day!

That's *Amazing!*

Especially
considering they fly
thousands of miles.

Hummingbirds migrate to the United States
and Canada to find a mate.

And to have baby Hummies.

The male Hummingbird tries to impress the female Hummingbird with amazing courtship dives!

He can reach speeds of over 55 miles per hour, which make it the fastest animal on Earth!

That's Amazing!

The male Hummingbird also shows off his feathers and colorful gorget.

23

THE TINIEST NESTS!

The Hummingbird's nest is tiny! It is about the size of a quarter.

The female Hummingbird will build a nest made of twigs and plants held together with spider's silk.

THE TINIEST EGGS!

The Hummingbird's eggs are
smaller than jelly beans! They
weigh less than a paper clip.

The babies hatch
in 2 weeks.

THE TINIEST BABIES!

Baby Hummingbirds weigh less than a dime.

That's *Amazing!*

They hatch with their eyes closed and almost no feathers. In 3 weeks Hummingbirds will have a full set of feathers.

Baby
Hummingbirds
are called
nestlings.

The Mama
Hummingird feeds
them insects and
nectar.

At just 2 weeks old Baby Hummingbirds start flapping their wings.

They are practicing to fly!

That's *Amazing!*

In 30 days Baby Hummingbirds are ready to fly!

That's Amazing!

WANT TO ATTRACT HUMMINGBIRDS TO YOUR YARD?

They are fun to watch and easy to attract.

FOLLOW THESE 3 EASY STEPS:

1
Get a Hummingbird Feeder

2
Get Hummingbird Flowers

3
Get a Water Fountain

STEP 1

GET A HUMMINGBIRD FEEDER!

Feeders are one of the best ways to attract Hummingbirds to your yard.

They love the flowers and the color red. Get a red feeder with flowers on it.

Be sure to clean the feeder 2 to 3 times a week to keep it safe for your Hummingbirds.

Photography by Barbara Caballero VanMatre

THE BEST SUGAR WATER RECIPE FOR FEEDERS!

1 cup refined white table sugar

4 cups water

Pour into a bowl and stir until sugar is dissolved

Rinse feeder with hot water

Pour sugar water nectar into feeder

(Refrigerate extra nectar)

STEP

GET FLOWERS HUMMINGBIRDS LOVE!

Petunia

Bleeding Heart

Zinnia

Cardinal

Butterfly Bush

Fox Glove

Trumpet Creeper

Salvia

Columbine

Bee Balm

Lantana

35

GET A WATER FOUNTAIN!

STEP  **3**

**Hummingbirds love to fly through
water and take baths.**

They like gentle flow fountains, bubblers and misters.

♥ GOOD JOB, KIDS! ♥

Now you know how to attract Hummingbirds to your yard.

 IN **3** EASY STEPS!

Kids! Want to Track Hummingbirds and Report Sightings?

View Hummingbird Migration Tracking Map!

Go to: Hummer-News.com

Take photos of your Hummingbirds and submit your favorite for PHOTO OF THE DAY!

Colorado

Lucia, 7

Michigan

Kimmy, 9

Texas

Max, 8

Featured on the Website & Facebook

Go to:
Hummer-News.com 39

FOR HUMMINGBIRD FUN!
GO TO
🖤HUMMER-NEWS.COM🖤

- Find out more about Hummingbirds!
- See Photos
- Free Coloring Pages
- Submit your Hummingbird Photo of the Day!

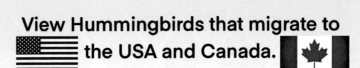

View Hummingbirds that migrate to the USA and Canada.

40